BREATHING TRUTH

BREATHING TRUTH

Quotations

from

Jalaluddin Rumi

Selected and translated by Muriel Maufroy

*To Rene
With Rumi's blessings
and much Love
Muriel December 2003*

**Sanyar Press
London**

First published 1997 by Sanyar Press - London

Copyright © Muriel Maufroy 1997

The right of Muriel Maufroy to be identified
as the author of this work has been asserted
by her in accordance with the Copyright, Designs
and Patents Act 1988

British Library Cataloguing in Publication Data
A catalogue record for this book is available from the British Library

ISBN 09529725 0 6

Cover illustration, from the dome of a 13th
century mosque - Karatay Museum, Konya, Turkey

Photograph by Delphine Barraclough

Printed in Malta by Interprint Ltd.

To Jean Gibson,

and to Effendi.

"The night and darkness of this world pass away; the light of these words is becoming increasingly more intense."
          Fihi-ma-fihi - 49 -

Acknowledgements

All the quotations in this book are based on the French translations by Eva de Vitray-Meyerovitch from the original Persian. Thanks to her monumental achievement - carried out in collaboration with Persian scholars - Western readers can have access to the whole of Rumi's work. I am deeply grateful to her for this gift.

My thanks to my friends, Robbie Lamming, Isabelle de la Taille, Kayhan Alsaç, Nuran Gungorencan, Nigel Watts and Jane Wisner, for their help and support.

Contents

Foreword	ix
Preface	xiii
Introduction	xv
The Quest	1
Mirror	19
Purification	37
Teacher	55
Beyond Time, Beyond Space	73
Prayer	91
Heart	109
Love	127
Fire	145
Suffering	163
Intoxication	181
One	199
Wonderment	217
Silence	235
Annihilation	253
Death	271

Foreword

Our material civilisation has reached its turning point. Earth can no longer contain humankind. Man travels in space, dives into the depths of the universe and attempts to solve the unsolved secrets of creation to their smallest details. But at the same time he has buried himself under a flood of material desires.

While racing in space he has neglected himself, forgetting who he is. Moral and religious values have been eroded by a destructive force. Humankind, which has developed materially to such a high degree, is being severed from its own nature, made prisoner of an artificial way of life. Desires rooted in passion have grown out of all proportion; they have become so wild that they know no boundaries. Man's spiritual world and its moral values are quietly heading for ruin. The monster of insatiable desires within us has grown far too strong and is out of control. We should be in service. Instead we are being dragged towards a catastrophe.

It is time that we grab hold of and control the monster. Man needs to come back to himself, he needs to experience his own nature. This need has never been so urgent. In order to succeed in this turning back, it is essential that man recognises his own truth. Ali, the Prophet Mohammed's son-in-law, said: "He who knows himself knows his God." In other words, he who does not know himself cannot know his God.

Those who have attained knowledge of the truth of man teach the truth of man. They are the Prophets and the saints of God. Fully realised teachers are all inheritors of the Prophets. Mevlana Jalaluddin Rumi is the highest of all saints. He is God's sun, the sun of life rising from eternity. He is the light of God's grace. He is the one who illuminates the hearts. He is the divine mercy that embraces the whole of humanity and the whole of life. Surrendering to Him is the real salvation and freedom, the freedom to experience the truth of the spirit and the unrevealed.

Mevlana Jalaluddin Rumi is like a great mountain on which divine guidance and light have focused. A magnificent mountain beyond horizons and above clouds. He is a living volcano of divine love, the impact of which will be felt until the Day of Judgement.

It is impossible for us to fully comprehend the truth of Mevlana. What we know to be "Mevlana" are His cries. These cries mean life. They are the visible lava that flowed out of the volcano, but then solidified. Can we enter the volcano? Can we keep our eyes on the sun? What we know of "Mevlana" are the roses of His art, the fragments of the light of His heart. Books and words about Mevlana are like attempts to fit an ocean into a container.

To reach a better understanding of Mevlana we need to dive into the sea of His love and to be with Him. Mevlana is the divine truth itself. The beauty of the secret resides in its secrecy. Each blossoming petal of a rosebud offers a different beauty, a different fragrance. To deserve the love of the rose one needs to be a nightingale: everything is for the rose. Everything is for the love of Mevlana. He who loves Mevlana, the lover of God, becomes a beloved of God.

My dear "daughter", Muriel, has brought together here torches set ablaze by the divine light of Mevlana. She has polished this book with the sparks of her heart and offered it to us. I congratulate her with all my heart.

al-Haj Sheikh Hüseyin Top
Sertariq* of the Mevlevi Order
Istanbul, January 1997

Sertariq represents the second authority within the Mevlevi Order. Appointed by the *Maqam Celebi* - a descendant of Rumi and the head of the Mevlevi Order - he is the link between the *Celebi* and the other sheikhs, and is the spiritual teacher of the Order.

Preface

This book is not an attempt to force Rumi's work and poetry into a rigid structured frame. It is an attempt to express the jewel-like quality of Rumi's work with its thousand facets, each sending back the Light from a different angle. Rumi often uses the metaphor of the mirror and his poetry is itself like a series of mirrors reflecting one another into infinity. In these reflections we can sometimes catch a glimpse of the Friend as well as of ourselves.

"You showed Your face in a thousand mirrors;
in each mirror You appear.
One single Sun shimmers in a thousand panes of glass."

This book consists of sixteen chapters, each of which represents one of Rumi's themes. Within each theme appear the multiple and often contradictory aspects of the various steps on the "Way". For Rumi will not allow us to sit comfortably in our spiritual clichés. Again and again he will surprise us, shock us out of our certainties and our dramas, pulling the carpet from under our feet so that, at last, we realise that Truth is not something to be caught once and for all, but that It is alive and therefore ever changing. Rumi wants us to know that Truth is a constant birth in us and around us and that what is a contradiction on the level of the mind is One on the level of the soul in an eternal breathing.

Introduction

Rumi's life is generally well known from the increasing number of those who, during the last fifteen or twenty years, have discovered this great Sufi poet, perhaps the greatest mystic poet of all times. What is often less known is how and when this immense work of his came to be. In fact the whole work of Rumi revolves around one meeting, his meeting with Shams-i-Tabriz in 1244 in Konya. But let's put this encounter in its context.

Rumi was born in 1207 in a small town near Balkh, in the province of Khorasan, then part of Persia, now Afghanistan. Rumi was about five when his father, a man of great intellectual and spiritual stature, first emigrated to Samarkand. A few years later, the family moved back to Balkh and it is only in 1219 that Rumi's father finally decided to go westward as the Mongol hordes were approaching. A year later Balkh was destroyed and razed by the men of Genghis Khan.

For nearly five years the family journeyed West, going first to Nishapur then Bagdad, then to Syria and Mecca, to finally settle in Laranda, about fifty miles south of Konya in Anatolia. Konya was then the capital of the Seljuk Empire and some years later, invited by the Sultan, Rumi's father moved to Konya. It is there that Rumi was to spend the rest of his life - except for a few years of study in Aleppo and Damascus - until his death in 1273.

Rumi was twenty two when he arrived in Konya. Two years later, his father died and Rumi succeeded him as a respected spiritual leader and teacher.

Through his father as well as from his life of travel and study he had acquired a formidable intellectual and spiritual wisdom. All that knowledge, however, was to be totally shattered when, in 1244, Rumi met Shams who introduced him to a deeper mystical knowledge which transformed him for ever.

What Shams imparted to Rumi was no ordinary transmission. It was a transmission from soul to soul which belonged to another dimension reaching far beyond the mind. But for this alchemical process to take place, an immense power had to be released: Rumi had to go through the most intense fire - and it almost destroyed him.

The meeting with Shams lasted only about three years, during which the pressure from Rumi's jealous disciples, forced Shams to leave. After much search, he was discovered in Damascus where Rumi sent his own son, Sultan Walad, to persuade him to return. But in December 1248, Shams disappeared again, this time for ever. Many believe he was murdered. Rumi was overcome by grief and it was thirteen years before he could at last find the peace which led him to compose his major work, the Mathnawi. Thirteen years of searing pain when, to the dismay of the religious orthodoxes of Konya, Rumi turned to dance, music and lyrical poetry as the only outlet for his grief and his love. It is during this period that Rumi founded the Mevlevi order in which the disciples perform the *sama*, the ceremony of the "whirling dervishes".

After the first disappearance of Shams Rumi had written the Ruba'iyat, (some 1600 quatrains), but the Diwan-i-Shams-i-Tabriz (2500 mystical odes) which poured out of him, was written after Shams's final disappearance.

Then in 1261 Rumi finally discovered in himself what he had so desperately been looking for in Shams, - his own immortal self.

"Although I glorified his beauty, I was the repository of all that beauty and grace."

The Mathnawi, a more sober work, now encompassing the whole of the human experience, could at last be written. Composed of six books, a total of 25,700 verses, the Mathnawi is often called in the Muslim world "the Koran in Persian".

One must not forget, however, Fihi-ma-Fihi, a treatise in prose, based on transcriptions of talks given by Rumi to his disciples. And finally mention must be made of Rumi's letters, most of them addressed to various officials in Konya.

As a whole, Rumi's work offers a complete view of a mystical teaching in the Sufi tradition. It is both monumental and magnificent, superb in its poetic imagery and extremely precise in its description of mystical states.

But even more importantly, this work, though written more than seven centuries ago, is now really reaching us. We are, it seems, at last able to listen to it.

The Quest

From the moment you entered this world of existence,
A ladder was put in front of you so you could escape.

Diwan

How shall we seek real knowledge? By renouncing knowledge.

How shall we seek salvation? By renouncing our own salvation.

How shall we seek Existence? By renouncing our existence.

MVI 823/824

Once you forget yourself, God remembers you: once you've become His slave, then you are free.

M III 3076

This quest is blessed; your seeking destroys the obstacles on the Way to God.
Your seeking is the key to what you seek, this quest is your army and the victory of your banners.

M III 1442/1443

Even if you are without means continue your search; on the way to Him, what need is there of means?

M III 1446

Don't look at your form, however ugly or beautiful.
Look at love and at the aim of your quest.
...**O** you whose lips are parched, keep looking for water.
Those parched lips are proof that eventually you will reach the source.

M III 1438/1440

Man is eyes, the rest is only flesh:

But the true eyes are those that see the Friend;

...

Merge the whole of yourself in your eyes,

Go towards the vision, go towards the vision,

go towards the vision.

M I 1406/M VI 1463

The time for staying at home is over,

It is time to enter the garden.

The dawn of happiness has risen,

the moment of union and vision is now.

Diwan - Ode 473 -

Even if He bars all the roads and passage-ways,
He will show you a hidden path unknown to all others.
When killing a ewe with his knife, the butcher doesn't forsake his victim: doesn't he take it with him after the killing?

Diwan - Ode 765 -

At every instant the heart hears this call from the blazing sun:"Renounce the torch of the earth and gain the torch of beyond."
Since you are serving the Beloved, why hide?
Gold shines always brighter from the wounds inflicted by the goldsmith.
Overwhelmed by the eternal Wine,
The heart was reciting joyfully:"The wine may tear my life away, it will give me another life."

          Diwan - Ode 538 -

How could you reach the pearl by only looking at the sea? If you seek the pearl, be a diver: the diver needs several qualities: he must trust his rope and his life to the Friend's hand, he must stop breathing, and he must jump head first.

Fihi ma fihi - 50

The difference between birds and intelligent men is that birds fly with their own wings in a certain direction, whilst intelligent men fly from all directions on the wings of their aspirations.

Fihi-ma-fihi - 71

Your desire for an illusion is like a wing.
This wing will take you to Reality.

....

Preserve the wing; do not feed the desire,
this wing of desire will take you to Paradise.
People think they are enjoying themselves: in reality they are tearing their wings apart for the sake of an imaginary form.

M III 2135- 2137-38

In this narrow cage, your soul has long trembled
Yet, in this doorless house, you are like a wingless bird.
The bird from heaven drops to the earth,
Its lament will eventually open the door of mercy.
Beat your wings against the door and against the roof;
this is the key.

Diwan - Ode 791

While walking with my Beloved I passed through a rose garden;
Out of ignorance, I looked at the flowers.
My Beloved said to me: Shame on you!
My face is here and you look at flowers!

Ruba'iyat

My Beloved said to me: "If you want to buy the kisses of each beloved, buy them from me."
I asked her: "With gold?" She answered: "What would I do with gold?" I asked: "With my soul?" She answered: "Yes, yes."

Rubai'yat

Mirror

Leave all worries behind and make your heart totally pure,
like the face of a mirror with no image or design.
Once your heart is cleansed of all images, it will contain them all.

Diwan - Ode 455 -

Do you know why the mirror of your soul reflects nothing?

Because its face has not been cleansed of rust.

M I 34

For a long time I searched for the image of my soul
but there was no one to reflect it.
After all, what is a mirror for? It is to reveal to each one
of us who he is and what he is.
The mirror of the soul is nothing else but the face of
the Friend; the face of the Friend belongs to our spiritual
home.

                                                    M II 93/96

Layer upon layer of rust has tarnished your heart,

making it blind to the mysteries...

When you dwell in sin and make a habit of evil...

Rust starts corroding the mirror.

II 3371 - 3378 - 3381

Once the mirror of your heart is clear and pure, you will see images beyond this world of water and clay. You will see both the image and the Maker of images, both the carpet of the kingdom and Him who lays the carpet.

M II 72/73

O man ensnared by time, I was a hidden treasure,
I wanted this treasure of goodness and magnificence
to be known.
I offered you a mirror; its face is the heart, its back is
the world.

Diwan

He who possesses the Heart becomes a mirror with six faces; through him God looks towards the six directions.

M V 874

The mirror shines through the veil, imagine how it will be once the mirror is unveiled!

M IV 3268

His signs are in the heart: outside the heart are the signs of the signs.

True orchards and gardens are in the very core of the soul; the image outside is like the image in running water.

....

True gardens and fruit are in the heart: their beauty is reflected on this world of water and earth.

M IV 1362-1363-1365

The beautiful are mirrors of His beauty:
the love they inspire reflects our true desire
which is for Him.

           M VI 3181

A friend of Joseph came to visit him. Joseph asked: "What did you bring me?" The friend said: "What could I bring you that you do not possess or might need? Nothing is more beautiful than your face. I brought you a mirror."

What is there that God doesn't possess or might need? To God you must bring a shining heart for Him to see Himself.

Fihi-ma-fihi 50

O you who are a copy of the divine Book,

You who are the mirror of the royal beauty,

Nothing exists in the world but you.

Search within yourself for what you desire: it is you.

Ruba'iyat

You saw your own image in the mirror of my form and you stood up in a rage to fight against yourself.

Like the lion who fell into the well because he imagined his reflection to be his enemy.

M VI 734/735

O you who see an ugly reflection in your uncle's face, it is not your uncle who is ugly, it is you; do not flee from yourself!

Believers are mirrors to each other...

M I 1327/1328

The lover cannot be anyone but the beloved: at every moment he bows down to himself; he bows to the mirror in order to see the face.

M VI 2259/60

I said: "O my heart, look for the universal Mirror, go towards the Sea. You won't reach your goal through the river alone."

...

I saw that you were the universal Mirror in all eternity: I saw my own image in your eyes.
I said: "At last I have found myself: in His eyes I have found the Way of Light."

M II 97 - 100/101

Purification

Purify yourself and become dust

So that from your dust flowers can grow.

Diwan - Ode 251 -

He whose soul is heavy with sin is like the dregs
at the bottom of the glass.
Once its dregs has been cleared, the soul rises
to the surface.
Don't stir the mud ceaselessly if your want your water
to become pure, your dregs to clear out, your pain to
recede.
The soul is like a flame whose smoke hides its
radiance;
When there is too much smoke, there is no light in
the house.
Dissipate the smoke, then you will enjoy the flame.

Diwan - Ode 26

You are a pearl hidden in a handful of straw mixed with mud.

Wash this mud from your face, O you whose face is beautiful, and see what happens!

You are the son of a king, you are the one before whom Gabriel bows.

.....

You are a mountain: seek in it the goldmine.

Diwan -Ode 844 -

We are a haystack, the wheat entangled with the hay;
Through the reviving wind, disentangle the wheat from the hay,
Let the sorrow go to the sorrow, the joy to the joy,
Let the mud go to the mud, and the heart rise to heaven.

Diwan - Ode 11 -

Let's admit I am a bad thorn, but the thorn grows for the sake of the rose.

...

Love and thanksgiving mingle with complaint, Peace keeps company with troubles.

Diwan - Ode 2 -

I run to You in fear of myself,

I am yours, don't give me back to myself.

Ruba'iyat

Once the blossoms are gone, the fruit becomes visible;

when one fades away, the other starts to grow.

How could bread give strength without being broken?

how could the grape give wine without being trodden?

M I 2930/2931

We are all shattered by You, Beloved, and why should this be strange?
You are the King and your grace consoles your servant.
I swear by the sweetness of your grace that all graces are your slaves,
That the bitterness coming from your grace is safe and beneficent.
...
Once your grace looks at sin with mercy,
this sin becomes adoration, then washes the soiled heart.

Diwan - Ode 908

God sent his prophets and his saints like a great pure Sea to cleanse all the small and impure rivers running into It. Once purified, the river remembers its original purity.

Fihi-ma-fihi - 8 -

Leave all your worries behind, let your heart be pure,
Like the face of the mirror, without images and without design;
Once free from images, it contains them all.

Diwan - Ode 455 -

They said to him: "Do stop crying or your sight will suffer,

For the eye becomes blind when tears overflow."

He answered: "If my two eyes at last see this Face,

Each fragment of myself will become an eye and I won't regret having lost my sight.

But if this eye is deprived of His sight,

Then it is better for me that an eye unworthy of Him becomes blind."

Diwan - Ode 3 -

Man is great. In him everything is written, but veils and darkness obscure his reading and prevent him from seeing the treasures which shine within himself.

Fihi-ma-fihi - 11 -

I am astonished to see him who is searching for purity, quiver at the moment of polishing, when handled roughly.

M III 4008

Be without sensations, without ears, without thought, in order to hear God's call: "Come back".

M I 568

Give only pure wine to the friends of purity;

.....

To God's lovers, give only God's Wine.

O you who are made naked on the Way,

clothe yourself with sunrays!

One doesn't offer a tunic to those who are

stripped on the Way of Love.

Diwan - Ode 917 -

Your desire for an illusion is like a wing.
This wing will take you to Reality.

M III 2135

Teachers

Don't look for help from someone other than yourself.

The remedy for your wound is the wound itself.

Diwan - Ode 425 -

The saints come to the rescue of this world when hearing from everywhere the moans of the oppressed.
They run towards them like God's mercy.
These fortresses against weakness,
these doctors of hidden disease,
Are pure love, pure justice, pure mercy; like God they are unstained and impregnable.

M II 1933/1936

If you do not possess the staff of caution and discrimination, use the eyes of him who sees.
If there is no staff of caution and discrimination, do not wander on the road without a guide.

M III 277-278

I asked: "Who is the guide who will take me to the Friend?"

He answered: "You must make the first step, then we will guide you."

Fihi-ma-Fihi - 64 -

Leave behind what is only a fragment of the heart
and look for the perfect heart; of this fragment,
the perfect heart will make a mountain.

M III 2271

Through the company of saints you become a saint. Whether rock or marble, once you have reached the heart of a saint, you will become a jewel.

M I 721/722

The disciple makes his heart a torn veil full of holes and presents it to the Wise.
The veil laughs through a hundred mouths; each mouth is an opening for the Master.

M II 1581/1582

Unless you become dust under the feet of a Master,
You cannot lead the army of the souls;
Unless you free yourself from "me" and "us",
You cannot befriend the angels.

Rubai'yat

I come and give you my life on loan. You say: "Don't bother. Go away."

I obey and take my leave. You say: "Come near, you idiot."

Diwan - Ode - 5 -

The presence of a friend of God is a book and more. The book of the Sufi is not made of ink and letter. It is only a heart as white as snow.

M II 158/159

He aimed at the form of the Perfected Man; in reality it is God that he reached.

M II 1178

Do not look at the Fakir seeking a treasure
as a treasure hunter: he is the treasure.
How could the lover be other than the beloved?

M VI 2259

Once "dead to the world and alive in God"
God's servant becomes God's shadow. Seize
the hem of his garment without wavering
in order to be saved at the end of time.
This shadow is the form of the saints
guiding us towards the light of the divine Sun.

                                                M I 423/425

When I love one of my servants, I am his ear so that he hears through Me; I am his eye so that he sees through Me; I am his tongue so that he speaks through Me.

Fihi-ma-fihi -28 -

He who possesses the Heart becomes a mirror with six faces: through him God looks towards the six directions. Whoever dwells in this world of the six directions, God looks at him only through the mediation of the Perfected Man.

If God dismisses you, He does it for the sake of the Perfected Man; and if He accepts you, it is also because of him.

M V 874/876

Never try to be a guide, stay a mere disciple.

To guide others is only an obstacle on the way.

Diwan - Ode 499 -

Beyond time, Beyond space

Once stifled in a single form, everything - even Paradise and the rivers of Eden - is ugly.

M IV 2383

All lovers look for signs: their love leads them only towards Him who is without signs.

Diwan - Ode 980 -

Did you see, did you hear from where I took you, to where I am taking you?

I will not leave you here either. I will take you beyond this earth, to a sweet earth, to a heaven you cannot even fathom; this heaven expands the soul in joy.

Letter 39

...know the true definition of yourself: it is essential. Once you know the definition of yourself, O you dust-sifter, flee from this definition and reach Him who is without definition.

M V 565/566

He has afflicted you from every direction in order to pull you back to the Directionless.

Diwan - Ode 368 -

When for a time you escape time, then dependency disappears; you become familiar with that which knows no dependence.

M III 2075

Be careful not to regret the past.

Be a Sufi, don't talk of the past.

You are the son of the moment, you are young,

you have vanquished time.

This short present moment must not be wasted.

Ruba'iyat

Our existences are only non-existence:
You are the absolute Being who makes these ephemeral things manifest.
We are lions heralded on blazing banners:
your hidden breath unfolds us from moment to moment.

M I 602-603

How is it that you do not know the way home
since you were born in this house of union?
....
You were kings and princes of royal blood, from the
beginning, and rightfully,
Though you are now moaning like beggars.

                                       Diwan - Ode 801 -

The heart intoxicated with the Beloved, what does it know of the road, of the stop, or of the distance long or short?
"Long" or "short" belong to the body: the journey in spirit is of another kind.
...
The journey in spirit is not of Time or Space.

M III 1977/1978-1980

The saint keeps within himself the infinite form without form of the Unseen reflected in the mirror of his own heart.

M I 3486

No wonder the spirit doesn't remember its previous dwelling,

...

This world, like sleep, hides the spirit, like clouds hide the stars.

M IV 3632/3633

This world is the dream of him who sleeps: the
dreamer imagines it is lasting
Until suddenly the dawn of Death breaks and he
finds himself free from the darkness of illusion and error.
Then seeing his eternal home, he will laugh at the
sorrows he endured.

M IV 3654-3655

Love has filled the six directions of the universe
with beauty
Yet we must leave behind the six directions.

Ruba'iyat

You are like the wind, at times hot, at times cold:
Go where heat and cold are no more.

Diwan - Ode 355 -

To be close to God does not mean climbing up or down; to be close to God means to escape from the prison of existence.

M III 4514

Prayer

The aim of prayer is to keep you always in the state you were in during prayer. Asleep or awake, writing or reading, whatever you do, you must never be without the remembrance of God.

Fihi-ma-fihi - 45 -

Day and night all creatures are revealing God; some are conscious of it, others not.

...

He who acknowledges God bears witness of Him always, but he who denies God also bears witness of Him.

Fihi-ma-fihi - 46 -

The ability to receive is not a necessary condition for divine generosity.
It is His generosity which is the necessary condition for receiving; generosity is the kernel, receptivity the shell.

M V 1537-1538

All night God calls us:

"Arise, use this time, O poor man,

Or after death, once your soul is separated

from your body,

You will have regrets.

                                            Diwan - Ode 313

The prayer of a sheikh is not like other prayers: he is annihilated and his words are the words of God.
Since God begs from Himself, how could He reject His own prayer?

> M V 2243-2244

Prayer and the response to prayer both come from You. It is You who first give the desire to pray; it is You who, in the end, give the response to prayers.

M IV 3499-3500

Atoms plead and moan in prayer.

Lightning hits them; dazzled they fall mute.

Diwan - Ode 33 -

In your prayer raise a shattered hand: God's tenderness runs towards him who is shattered.

M V 493

Through saying so many prayers, I have become a prayer.

Diwan - Ode 942 -

Show me your face, O Thou, who art like a torch
While I caress Thee, I neither fast or pray,
While I am with Thee, my sin is a prayer,
When without Thee, my prayer is a sin.

Ruba'iyat

The soul of prayer is not only its form: prayer prepares for the absorption into God and for the loss of consciousness when all forms remain outside. Then there is no more room in the soul, even for a pure spirit like Gabriel.

Fihi-ma-fihi - 3 -

Flesh and blood are not the enemy; the enemy is the hostile thought within you; to chase away the enemy you only have to chase away the thought through thanksgiving.

Fihi-ma-fihi - 68 -

Thought occupies itself with past and future; once freed of both, the obstacle is vanquished.

M II 177

While praise and prayer were given to you as gifts, in prayer, your heart became full of pride.

You saw yourself speaking with God. Many are those who became separated from God through such an opinion.

Even if the king sits down with you on the floor, know yourself and show more respect.

M II 339/341

...when your carnal soul wishes to complain, act in the opposite direction, give thanks to God and make such efforts that His love springs from within yourself... to give thanks without motive is to seek God's love.

Fihi-ma-fihi - 68 -

Many prayers are loss and destruction; in His mercy, God doesn't listen to them.

M I 140

Heart

Stop desiring the two worlds
The heart's dwelling contains Him only.

Diwan - Ode 123 -

The heart is the dwelling of safety, O my friends, in it are fountains and rose gardens within rose gardens.
Turn towards the heart and go forward, O night traveller; there you'll find trees and streams of running water.

M III 515-516

His signs are in the heart: outside are only the signs
of the signs.
True orchards and gardens are in the very core of
the soul; the image outside is like the image in running
water.

...

True gardens and fruit are in the heart: this outside world
reflects their beauty.

                                           M IV 1362/1365

God put a lock on the heart and sealed it.

You want to open that door? Then sink into pain.

Diwan - Ode 858 -

The lover has a wounded heart because he has the audacity of a lion:
He whose heart is so brave, how could he flee from the wounds of the heart?

Diwan - Ode 794 -

Since without rest He moves the heavens, O my heart,
be like a star and don't look for rest.
If you seize a branch, how will He let you hold on to it?
Wherever you tie yourself, He will break that tie.

M VI 914-915

Everyone is astonished and I too am amazed:
He whom no one can contain, how is it that He can
be contained in the heart?

Diwan - Ode 806 -

...know that the mirror of the heart is boundless...
the heart is with God, or indeed, it is Him.

M I 3488/3489

The heart possesses the seal of Solomon, it controls the five senses; for the heart, the five external senses are easy to control and the five internal ones are under its command.

M I 3574-3575

The shrine in the hearts of saints, it is there that everyone bows down, it is there that God dwells.

Aflaki * - volume I -

---

*Rumi's hagiographer

That which God told the rose and which made her beauty unfold,
He told my heart and made it a hundred times more beautiful.

M III 4129

I cried: "The drunken heart, where is it going?"

"Be silent", the King of kings answered: "it is coming towards us."

Diwan - Ode 898 -

The Sun knows a way, hidden, towards the ruby in the mine. Through Its heat the Sun changes the stone into a ruby. But stones and rubies have no knowledge of this.

It is the same with the Sun of divine Mercy towards the heart of the believer, the hidden jewel in the mine of his body. The stone of the body and the ruby of the heart know nothing of this secret way; they perceive only what reaches them.

Letter 42

The disciple makes his heart a torn veil full of holes
and wears it before the Wise.
The veil laughs at him through a hundred mouths;
each mouth betrays him to the Master.
...through these openings, He sees your thoughts:
your heart bears witness of your thoughts.

M I 1581/1588

A hundred flames shine in the eyes.
They come from this finest part of the heart
where fire dwells.
How strange! In this burning place
There are so many roses, so much greenery,
so much jasmine.
Through this fire, the garden cools down
And water weds the flame.

Diwan -Ode 685 -

Your heart may have a thousand locks;

Do not fear: search for the shop of Love.

Love will unlock your heart.

Diwan - Ode 909 -

Love

Love is the universal order, we are the atoms; love is the ocean, we are the drops.

Love has offered us a hundred proofs; we are looking for reasons.

Through love, the heavens are ordered; without love, suns and moons are eclipsed,

Through love, what was bent is made straight; without love, what was straight becomes bent

Diwan -Ode 2 -

Without love no one is entitled to enter into the presence of the Beloved.
They say: "What is love?" Answer: "Renounce your own will."

Diwan - Ode 455 -

If love has no purpose towards us, if it doesn't desire us,
What extravangance makes it ravish our hearts and minds?

Diwan - Ode 863 -

In the bloody veil of love, roses dwell.

...

Reason says: "These six sides of space are barred, there is no escape."

Love says: "There is a path; I trod it many times."

...

Reason says: "Do not put your foot here; in death there are only thorns."

Love answers: "The thorns are in you."

Keep silent, pull the thorn of existence out of your heart

And discover rose-gardens in your own soul.

Diwan - Ode 132 -

Love took away my sleep: this is what love does.

...

Love is like a black lion, starved and fierce

Drinking blood only from the hearts of lovers.

Love's tenderness seizes you and takes you towards the trap;

Once you are in the trap, it looks at you from afar

...

Love tortures and oppresses the innocents.

Those who fall into its hands cry like clouds,

Those who flee from it are frozen like the snow.

Diwan - Ode 919 -

Since the love for my Beloved filled my heart,

My groans have kept my neighbour awake.

My groans have now receded, my love has grown:

When kindled by the wind, fire gives no smoke

Ruba'iyat

Truly between two hearts there exists a window; hearts do not stay apart like bodies. The clay of the lamps cannot meet, but their light does.

Truly no lover is in search of union without his beloved also searching for this union.

...

When in your heart your love for God grows, know without the shadow of a doubt that God is loving you.

...

The thirsty man cries: "O delicious water,(where are you?)"

The water moans: "Where is the drinker of water?"

M III 4391-4393-4396-4398

None of these lovers' quests comes from them.
On this earth there is no seeker but Him.

Diwan - Ode 425 -

You are in love with your "state", you are not in love with me. You love me hoping to obtain a "state".

M I 1428

A love came which obscured all loves.

I burnt away: my ashes became life.

Yearning to be burnt again,

My ashes came back with a thousand faces.

Ruba'iyat

The Friend may leave me; He is not to blame.

I sit and wait for His next move.

Ruba'iyat

Look at the pain of love as divine grace.
Transient love is one of the ways to divine love.
He who goes to war for God gives his son a wooden sword,
For him to learn mastery and the wielding of the battle sword.
Love for a human being is like the wooden sword;
After trials, that love becomes love for God.
For years Zuleika loved Joseph;
In the end her love became divine love and she turned away from Joseph.

Diwan - Ode 27 -

The pure ruby may love itself or love the sun,

in reality there is no difference between these two loves:

both are only the radiance of the rising sun.

M V 2029/2030

In the heart of lovers, there is a pain no remedy can cure: neither sleep nor walk, nor food, nothing except the sight of the Friend, for the meeting with the Friend is the cure.

                                        Fihi-ma-fihi

You said: "Come! The spring garden is smiling,
There are torches, wine, beauty."
In that place where you are not, what is all this to me?
And in that place where you are, what good are
all these?

Ruba'iyat

Which pain, which affliction can be worse to the soul than to be without news of you?

Diwan - Ode 7 -

Fire

If you become flower, wither and burn joyfully

So that from your burning, light may spring.

Let your burning change you into ashes,

Your ashes will become the philosopher's stone.

Diwan - Ode 251 -

On the fire like a cauldron, look for yourself,
Bring yourself to the boil, do not flee in all directions;
Your goal is the precious stone. Go and search for it;
This fire will transmute you into a precious stone.

Rubai'yat

O love, like a temple of fire! You who took

a form and a body,

You who looted the caravan of the heart,

give us a moment of rest.

From dusk to dawn, all my nights are spent

on fire, burning.

Diwan - Ode 5 -

Fire is used when the pot is cold, not when it is boiling.

M III 4383

We are those burnt ones who, out of desire for the burn,
Renounce the Water of Life and go in search of fire.

Diwan - Ode 785 -

Be like the moth giving up its life;

...

Let yourself be consumed in this flame, illumine your heart and your soul. Clothe yourself with a new body and leave the old one.
Why do you fear the fox, you who belong to the lion race?

...

The eternal friend will come and open the door of joy,
This friend is the key, you are the lock.

Diwan - Ode 638 -

When, through a veil, God reveals Himself to the mountain, trees, flowers, bushes are transfigured. But when He reveals Himself without veil, the mountain is shattered and reduced to ashes.

Fihi-ma-fihi - 9 -

Yesterday fire whispered to the ear of the smoke:
"The aloe can't bear me, yet it feels happy with me;
It knows how to appreciate me, it offers me thanks".
For the aloe has found a gift in its own annihilation.
The whole of the aloe was made of knots,
The joy of annihilation dissolved all its knots.
O my friend in love with the flame, be welcome.

Diwan - Ode 863 -

Since the love of my Beloved filled my heart,

My groans have kept my neighbours awake.

My groans have now receded, my love has grown.

When kindled by the wind, fire gives no smoke.

Ruba'iyat

A hundred flames shine in the eyes.

They come from that finest part of the heart where

fire dwells.

How strange! In this burning place there are so many

roses, so much greenery, so much jasmine.

Through this fire the garden cools down

And water weds the flame.

Diwan - Ode 685 -

The soul which cannot endure fire and smoke won't find the Secret.

Diwan - Ode 887 -

If your knowledge of fire comes only from words, ask to be cooked; do not dwell in the certainty acquired through others.

There is no real certainty before burning. You want this certainty? Then enter fire.

M II 860-861

Leap into the flame when His torch is burning. You won't be able to live without the flame once you know the ecstasy of the burn.

                              Diwan - Ode 566 -

The weaning from this world, wasn't it like fire?
The pilgrims are gone and in reality this weaning was Light.
Know that the Candle of Spirit never ceases to grow : contrary to the candle of flames which appears like Light but burns its friend; the Candle of Spirit appears like fire but, to those who visit It, is as sweet as roses.

...

To those who stand in the presence of God, the spark of pure and noble Light is shining; to those who are afar from God, this spark is like fire.

M III 4372/4375

O candle, you seem to have the qualities of the Sufis!
For you have six attributes which belong to the people of Purity:
Sleepless nights, a radiant face, pallor,
A burning heart, tears in the eyes and alertness.

Ruba'iyat

Smoke always comes from kindling, not from blazing fires.

M III 3569

Suffering

O my soul, don't flee from the pain inflicted by the Beloved.

Pain will make you ripe. Without pain you'll stay unripe.

Diwan - Ode 963

Nobody has ever fled from pain without receiving something worse in exchange.

Diwan

God said: "Do not grieve when losing what escapes you," when the wolf comes and devours your sheep; This misfortune deters great misfortunes; this loss prevents huge losses.

M III 3264-3265

If you have suffered something painful, it is mostly due to your spiritual attainment, for your happiness and your salvation.

...

His eternal grace always transforms pain into remedy, loss into gain.

...

When told by their enemies that God had abandoned them, prophets and saints would say:"We are weak, it is true, and because of our carnal soul we are miserable, we moan in despair. Yet in the depth of our soul we possess a solid trust; for we are aware of God's promise: in the end, He will change this poison into sugar, our darkness into light; He will make straight our battered destiny."

Letter 45

He has afflicted you from every direction, In order to pull you back to the Directionless.

Diwan - Ode 368 -

All pains come from your desire for the unattainable. If you have no desire, you will have no pain. But deep within, the call of desire and thought cannot disappear; such a temptation disappears only in the rapture in God

Fihi-ma-fihi - 31 -

He who is without pain is a scoundrel, for to be without pain is to say: "I am God."

M II 2521

Through birth you appeared in this world of the four directions. It is also through birth that you can escape from your chains.

But that birth is not of water or earth; only the pure-hearted man can know it. This birth is compulsory, that birth is willed...

The birth of the child tears apart the mother's womb, the birth of man shatters the universe.

Diwan -

The heart is like a vessel of light; The ocean of pain submerged it.

It became a warrior after having been a martyr a hundred times.

I love the waves of this ocean. I am both the feast and the sacrifice.

Diwan - Ode 583 -

Even when you tear its petals off one after another, the rose keeps laughing and doesn't bend in pain. "Why should I be afflicted because of a thorn? It is the thorn which taught me how to laugh."
Whatever you lost through fate, be certain that it saved you from pain.
A Sheikh was asked: "What is Sufism?" He said: "To feel joy in the heart when sorrow appears."

M III 3258/3262

If the thought of sorrow spoils your joy, yet it prepares you for joy.
Sorrow sweeps the house fiercely, emptying it of everything, then, coming from the Source of goodness, a new joy enters.
Sorrow chases away the withered leaves in the heart, then new green leaves can grow.
Sorrow uproots the previous joy, then a new delight springs from beyond.

M V 3678/3681

The lover of this world is like someone in love with a wall illuminated by sunrays; he doesn't realise that the radiance and the splendour do not come from the wall but from the sun; he gives his heart to the wall and when at sunset the rays of sun disappear, he is in despair.

M I 2801

We order you to journey on Our endless Path with these weak hands and feet. We know that your feet are too weak to tread this Path. Even in a hundred thousand years, you won't reach the resthouse. You are trying so hard to reach the goal that you will be exhausted, you will lose your strength and fall. Then God's grace will come and rescue you.

Fihi-ma-fihi - 17 -

Once the blossoms are gone, the fruit becomes visible;
when one fades away, the other starts growing.
How could bread give strength without being broken?
How could the grape give wine without being crushed?

M I 2930/2931

Since you saw the Friend near, why do you still have love for yourself?

...

Don't be stubborn, do not flee from happiness.

Diwan - Ode 638 -

O my friend who can't bear to be without this world, how can you bear to be without God?

M IV 3213

Intoxication

What does it matter that the jug and the gourd are shattered?
Trust Him who gives existence and provides drunkenness.

Diwan - Ode 1044 -

The Wine, pure drink, dissolves sorrows:
In the intoxicated soul, how could there be room
for sorrow?

> Diwan - Ode 489 -

Your love has prepared a feast for me;

Reason came and sat in a corner;

The wine was laughing in the cup,

The jug was crying tears of blood.

The wine, archer of joy,

Has pierced the bird of sorrow with its arrows.

Diwan - Ode 508 -

My drunken heart belongs to the wine seller;

I have traded my soul for a cup.

When my soul and my heart fell in love with the wine,

I offered them both and became free of sorrow.

Ruba'iyat

If for one second you can comprehend the mysteries,
You will offer your life willingly.
As long as you are drunk with yourself, you will be darkness eternally;
Once intoxicated with Him, you will be awakened.

Ruba'iyat

When seeking the secret, go to those who are drunk:
He who is drunk and abandoned cannot keep secrets.

Diwan - Ode 927 -

...you are sin itself if, amidst the assembly of souls, you stay sober.

> Diwan - Ode 801 -

The heart intoxicated with the Beloved,
What does it know of the road, of the stop, or of a long or short journey?
"Long" or "short" belong to the body: the journey in spirit is of another kind.

M III 1977-1978

The intoxication of desire in this earthly world is
of little account compared with the intoxication of angels.
The intoxication of angels annihilates the intoxication
of men: how could the angel be tempted by desire?
Until you drink clear water, brackish water tastes sweet
to the lips, as sweet as the light in the eyes.
But a single drop of heavenly wine ravishes the soul
away from the cupbearers of this world.

                                                M III 820/823

Once I understood that love was with me always,

That its curls were in my hand,

Though yesterday I was drunk with wine,

Today it is the wine which is drunk within me.

Ruba'iyat

He who walks near my tomb becomes drunk:

Does he linger, his drunkenness becomes eternity.

Does he enter the sea, the sea becomes drunk.

Does he enter the earth, the tomb and the stone become drunk.

Ruba'iyat

Before there was ever a garden, a vine, a grape,
Our soul was drunk with eternal wine.

...

O cupbearer, intoxicate these people full of pride,
So that they learn what joy they have been missing.

Diwan - Ode 731 -

If from my dust, wheat grows,

If from this wheat, you make bread, this bread will make you drunk.

The dough and the baker will both become mad.

The oven will sing drunkards' songs.

My tomb will make you dance.

O brother, do not come without your drum.

At God's banquet, sadness is not fitting.

Diwan - Ode 683 -

We are both the mirror and the face,
We are drunk from the eternal cup.
We are the remedy and the cure,
We are both the Water of Life and the cupbearer pouring it.

Ruba'iyat

Wine is allowed to comfort ordinary people; it is not allowed for those seeking the Beloved.
Wine, for God's lovers, is the blood of their hearts; their eyes are fixed on the Way and the Destination.

M V 3485

The Wine of divine grace is boundless;
Only the cup limits it.

         Diwan - Ode 939 -

One

O you who have gone astray, why are you searching all over the world?
He is not outside you. Why search for Him?

Ruba'iyat

The moon gained light for embracing the night,
The rose was given fragrance for conspiring with
the thorn.

Ruba'iyat

When conflict rages within yourself, you imagine two armies face to face:
When there is no conflict within yourself, you know there is only one single army.

Diwan - Ode 458 -

How could the lover be other than the beloved? Every minute he bows before himself.

M VI 2259

What dazzles you when you look at beauty is the Light of the Sun filtering through the coloured glass.

...

Become used to the Light without the glass so that once the glass is shattered, the Light does not blind you.

M V 988-991

You gave form to this "I" and this "we" for You to
play the game of adoration with Yourself;
For all the "I's" to become one single soul,
submerged in the Beloved with You.

M I 1787-1788

The pure ruby may love itself or the sun,
in reality there is no difference between these two loves:
both are only the radiance of the rising sun.

M V 2029/2030

Love God for something other than Him, in order
to be at all time part of His bounty;
Or love God for Himself, for nothing else than Himself,
for fear of being estranged from Him.
Both quests and searches come from that same Source
where His heart ravishes hearts.

M III 4598/4600

There is the eye of the Sea and there is the foam.
Leave the foam behind and look with the eye of
the Sea.
Day and night foam is born out of the Sea: how strange!
You keep looking at the foam and not at the Sea!

M III 1270/1271

You are not one "you" only, O my friend: you are the sky and the deep sea.
This powerful "You", a thousand times greater,
is the ocean where a hundred "you's" are drowning.

M III 1303-1304

O people of purity wandering in this world,

Why have you gone astray for a single idol?

The one you are seeking in this world,

Seek him within yourself: you are this idol.

Ruba'iyat

He has come, he has come, he who never left.

This stream never lacked water.

He is the treasure of musk, we are his fragrance:

Have you ever known the musk without the fragrance?

Ruba'iyat

Your intelligence is split into a hundred busy tasks,
in thousands of desires, in large and small things.
You must unite these scattered parts with love and
become as sweet as Samarkand and Damascus.
Once you are unified, grain by grain, then you can be
stamped with the royal seal.

> M IV 3288/3290

The World of Unification is beyond the senses;
If you desire Unity, follow that direction.

M I 3099

Renounce all the faces in you heart

Until the Face without a face comes to you.

                                                          Ruba'iyat

You ask: "Where can I fly in order to find Him?"
But where can you fly where He is not?

Ruba'iyat

Wonderment

God's action appears sometimes one way, sometimes completely reversed. The work of the Spirit is nothing else but wonderment.

M I 312

It is as if a bird were perched on top of your head;

your soul trembles lest it should take flight.

You dare not move for fear of seeing it fly away,

You dare not breathe; you dare not cough...

...

Wonder is like this bird: it makes you silent; it closes

the lid on the pot and fills you with Love's boiling.

M V 3246/3250

This created human form

Is an image tied to a thread of sorrow.

Demon, angel or wild beast,

What is this magic He has created?

Rubai'yat

With the dawn of divine love,

The human soul takes flight,

Then with each breath

And without eyes, man sees the Friend.

Rubai'yat

In one single day and one single night, God deals with a hundred thousand things: He takes away a whole people, He separates those who were close and scatters each of them in a different country, then He raises the waves of the sea of destiny and reunites those who were separated.

Letter 38

No intelligence, no imagination could believe this story: that beyond this darkness, beyond this nourishing blood, another world, another food existed. Yet though this drop of sperm denied such a possibility, it could not help leaping out when forcibly ejected.

Letter 39

He who looks at the foam speaks of mystery, but he who looks at the sea is full of wonder.

He who looks at the foam expresses intentions, but he who looks at the sea makes his heart the sea.

He who looks at the flakes of foam makes plans, but he who looks at the sea has no will.

He who looks at the foam keeps busy, but he who looks at the sea is totally pure.

M V 2908/2911

You are both Existence and Nothingness,

All your joy, all your sorrow are Him.

You have no eyes to see this,

Or you would see that from head to toe you are Him.

Rubai'yat

Everyone is astonished and I am in wonder at this:
He whom no one can contain, how is it He is contained in the heart?

> Diwan - Ode 806 -

He whispered to the ear of the rose and made her laugh;
He spoke to the stone, the stone became precious.
He sent a message to the body, the body became
spirit. He spoke to the sun, the sun blazed.
Again He whispers frightening words to the ear and
a hundred eclipses obscure the sun.
Imagine what He sang to the cloud to make tears stream
from its eyes.
Imagine what He sang to the earth to make it worried
and since then silent!

                                              M 1451/1455

In non-existence there are suns, and that which is sun here, is only a little star there.

...

Non-existence is God's workshop from where He is constantly producing gifts.

M V 1017-1024

Read one single page of our book,

And you will be filled with wonder.

Attend for one instant the lesson of the heart,

And your teaching will attract masters.

Rubai'yat

Sell cleverness and buy wonderment: cleverness is opinion, wonder is vision.

M IV 1407

The wonder is that colour came from the colourless: how is it that colour came to fight the colourless?

...

Since the rose is born from the thorn, and the thorn from the rose, why are they quarelling?
Or is it not really war but divine purpose and artifice, like the quarrels of merchants?
Or is it neither this nor that? Is it the perplexity? The treasure must be sought; this perplexity is the ruin where it is hidden.

M I 2470-2472/2474

The intellect was astonished; it said: "what is love and what is ecstasy? I wonder what is the most wonderful: separation from Him or union with Him?

                                                                        M II 4717

Keep silent, bathe in this wonder.

Renounce the secrets: this is the Secret.

Diwan - Ode 342 -

Silence

Be silent. It is without words that He makes everyone taste His Wine.

Diwan - Ode 765 -

I think of rhymes and my Beloved says to me: "Think of nothing but seeing Me.

......

What are words that you think of them? What are words?
Thorns in the edge surrounding the vine.
I shall bring confusion to words, sounds and speeches, so that, in their absence, I might talk with you."

M I 1727-1729/1730

To speak about Him is to close the window through which He reveals Himself: the mere act of speaking conceals Him.

M VI 699

I told my heart: "If you are able to speak,

Tell my beloved of my pain."

My heart answered: "When I am with the Beloved,

I have no words, I look at Him."

                                                    Rubai'yat

Keep silent in order to hear God's whisper.
There are a hundred thousand lives in
this whisper.

>>>>>>>>>>>>>>>>>>>>>>>>>>Diwan - Ode 233 -

As long as you stay silent, His words are your words;
as long as you do not weave, He is the weaver.

Diwan

Words and names are traps: sweet words are the sands absorbing the water of our soul.

M I 1061

Words can help polish the mirror of the heart,
Yet too many words will tarnish it.

Diwan - Ode 974 -

God said to the ear: "Be silent."

When the child is born, first he keeps silent, he is all ears.

For a while he must abstain from speech until he learns how to speak...

Since in order to speak, first you must hear, learn how to speak through listening.

M I 1622/1627

My heart weeps with the Friend's heart,

Such is silent eloquence!

I speak without moving my lips,

Since the jealous are listening, and since

I know that both tongue and ear are indiscreet,

I speak with my heart, for the heart is faithful.

Diwan - Ode 685 -

When Othman became Khalif, he went to the pulpit. People were waiting for his words. He stayed silent, looked at the people and brought down on them such a state, such an ecstasy, that they dared not move. They ceased to be conscious of each other. A hundred sermons couldn't have brought such result.

Fihi-ma-fihi - 31 -

Do not speak, for God knows best what is right.

Do not speak, in order to hear from the Speakers what was neither told nor explained.

Do not speak, in order to hear from the Sun what is not in books or in speeches.

Do not speak, so that the Spirit may speak for you.

M III 1304/1306

I said: "O you who unsettled my heart and soul,
I have no strength left to keep calm." He said at last:
"You are the drop of my ocean. Stop talking.
Drown and your soul, like a shell, will be filled
with pearls."

                              Diwan - Ode 1022 -

Words are a trap to capture the breath of Him whose lips are sweet.

M I 1189

Keep silent; bathe in this wonder.

Renounce the secrets: this is the Secret.

Diwan - Ode 342 -

Atoms plead and groan in prayer.

Lightning strikes them; dazzled they fall mute.

Diwan - Ode 33

Annihilation

To experience the day of Resurrection, first you must die.

This is why everyone has taken the wrong direction, for they fear non-existence while, in reality, it is the refuge.

M VI 821-822

Since you are seeking the desire and the will of the Friend,
Seeking your own desire is for you illicit.

Diwan - Ode 374 -

I come from this Soul from which all souls come,
I am from the city of those who have no city.
The path to this city is endless.
Go, lose everything you have; it is that which is everything.

Ruba'iyat

Yesterday fire whispered to the ear of the smoke:
The aloe can't bear me, yet it feels happy with me;
It knows how to appreciate me; it offers me thanks,
For the aloe has found a gift in its own annihilation.

Diwan - Ode 863 -

Each soul runs from poverty and destruction,

How sad! It is running away from happiness and joy.

No one can triumph before being destroyed

O Beloved! reconcile me with destruction.

Diwan - Ode 863 -

If you become December, you will feel the coming of spring. If you become night, you will know the coming of daylight.

M V 552

The tailor of time never sewed a coat for anyone,
Without then tearing it apart.

Diwan - Ode 869

As long as you have an "I" you won't be allowed in.
Once you are annihilated you will be treasured like
the apple of the eye;
Once you are purified from the two worlds,
You will be stamped with the seal of detachment.

                                                  Ruba'iyat

Don't be a drop, become an ocean.

If you want to be a sea, destroy the drop.

Ruba'iyat

Since you saw this spring, why didn't you become water?
Since you saw the Friend near, why do you still have love for yourself?
Since you are in the shop of the sweet-seller, why this bitter look?
Since you are swimming in the river of life, why are you dry and miserable?
Don't be stubborn, do not flee from happiness.
...
You are imprisoned in a net from which you can't escape,
Stop struggling! Stop struggling!

Diwan - Ode 638 -

You are a lover of God; when God comes, not one piece of your hair remains.

Before Him a hundred beings like you vanish: it seems, my friend, that you are in love with your own annihilation.

You are a shadow, in love with the sun: comes the sun, the shadow disappears.

M III 4621/4623

The stone is changed into pure ruby: the ruby possesses all the qualities of the sun,
and none of the stone: the whole ruby is filled with the sun.
Then if the ruby loves itself, this love is for the sun.
And if it loves the sun with all its soul, no doubt this love is for itself.

                                                        M V 2025/2028

A sun is hidden within the atom: suddenly the atom bursts open.

Heaven and earth crumble before this sun leaping out of ambush.

M VI 4580

You have endured many pains but you are still
under the veil for you must first die to yourself
and you have not.

...

The ship of self-consciousness, once totally shattered,
becomes like the sun on the vault of the sky.
Since you didn't die, your pain has been prolonged.

M VI 723 -729/730

O you who are sincere, if you want this Reality

to be unveiled, choose death and tear up the veil;

Not a death leading to the tomb, but a death which

is transmutation and leads you into the Light.

M VI 738-739

The Beloved has infused all my cells.
Of me only a name remains, all the rest is Him.

Ruba'iyat

Death

Death shatters the cage but doesn't wound the bird. How could death rough up the feathers of the eternal bird?

Diwan - Ode 215 -

The lion said to me: "You are a lovely gazelle. Go.
Why run after me so fast? I will devour you"
Aren't you a lion's son, hidden in a gazelle body?
I will free you of this guise.

Diwan - Ode 322 -

O body like a walnut, Love is your friend: your soul will seek your kernel and destroy your shell.

M V 1932

When walking in the grip of death,
Through the country of nothingness, I will
create a great tumult;
Nothingness will be astonished; nowhere
In the two worlds is there a lover like me.

Ruba'iyat

Reason shivers in the fear of death, but Love is full of audacity: the stone is no clod of earth; how could it fear rain?

M V 4225

The body is a narrow house: the soul within it is imprisoned: God destroys the house in order to build a royal palace.

M III 3555

Unless you become dust under the feet of a Master,
You cannot lead the army of the souls;
Unless you renounce "me" and "us",
You cannot befriend the angels.

Ruba'iyat

Endure your sorrow quietly; I am your remedy.
Don't look at someone else; I am your Friend.
When you are dead, do not say: "I was killed."
Be thankful; I am the prize for your blood.

Ruba'iyat

From Your love leaps the flame of youth;
In the heart springs the beauty of the soul.
You want to kill me? My blood is yours.
Death from the Friend is life.

            Ruba'iyat

The day my soul rises in heaven,

The cells of my body will be scattered.

With your finger write on my dust: "Rise up."

So that I rise from the tomb and my body lives again.

Ruba'iyat

If your life is not yet illuminated, you still have a few moments left: die to yourself like a man.

M V 1771

A man was saying: "This world would be a delight were it not for death to come."
Another said: "If death were not, this disorderly world wouldn't be worth a straw."
...
You thought that life was that which in reality is death; you have sown your grain on a barren land.

M V 1760/1763

For him who is in love with death and doesn't fear it, death becomes the friend of his heart.
When fear has vanished, indeed there is no death, only the appearance of death; in reality it is a happy emigration.

M III 4611/4612

Demolish the house...

Under it the treasure is buried; do not fear to destroy the house, do not stay inactive.

With one single treasure one can build a thousand houses without labour.

In the end this house will crumble by itself and the treasure will be found;

But it won't be yours; the spirit receives this divine gift as its salary for demolishing the house.

M IV 2540/2544

Like sea birds men come from the Ocean, the ocean of the soul.
How could the bird, born of this ocean, make this earth its home?

                              Diwan - Ode 463 -

When you see my corpse, do not cry: "Gone, gone."

For union and meeting will be mine.

Putting me in the grave, do not say: "Farewell, farewell."

The grave is a veil hiding the assembly of Paradise.

Diwan - Ode 911 -

Bibliography

- Odes Mystiques - Editions Klingsieck - Paris - 1973

- Le Livre du Dedans - Editions Sindbad - Paris - 1982

- Ruba'iyat - Editions Albin Michel - Paris - 1987

- Lettres - Editions Jacqueline Renard - Paris - 1990

- Le Mathnawi - Editions du Rocher - Monaco - 1990

In the garden this morning I picked some roses,
I was afraid the gardener would see me.
I heard him saying gently:
What are flowers! I give you the whole garden.

Ruba'iyat